Written by Alan MacDonald
Illustrated by Maïté Schmitt

Words to look out for ...

convince *VERB*
To convince someone is to persuade them about something.

habit *NOUN*
something that you do often

link *VERB*
To link things is to join them together.

minimum *ADJECTIVE*
least or smallest

reduce *VERB*
If something reduces or is reduced, it gets smaller in size or amount.

sensible *ADJECTIVE*
A sensible person or thing is wise or shows common sense.

Chapter 1

The Dragon family were having breakfast. Mrs Dragon was stirring a pan of hot chocolate with her tail. Grandpa Dragon was snorting fire to make toast. The twins, Frankie and Zuzu, were eating bowls of steaming porridge. The Dragons liked things hot.

The Dragons lived in a house on a hill, high above the rooftops of the town. People lived in the town ... and that was the problem.

"Ma, can we go out today?" asked Frankie.

"We'll only go down the hill," said Zuzu. "We want to see what the town is like."

"No good will come of it," warned Grandpa.

"Be sensible," said Mrs Dragon. "I've told you, dragons and people don't mix."

A sensible person or thing is wise or shows common sense.

The truth was the Dragons hardly ever left the house.

"Remember the time I went shopping in town?" asked Mrs Dragon. "I only said 'hello' and people screamed and ran away."

"It's difficult to convince people that we're friendly," said Grandpa.

"It's better to stay at home," agreed Mrs Dragon.

To convince someone is to persuade them about something.

"If we keep away from people, they keep away from us," said Grandpa.

Just then, a noise at the door made them all jump.

"What was that?" asked Mrs Dragon. None of them moved.

Something was scratching at the door, trying to get in.

"Maybe the post is here," said Frankie.

"Could it be a mouse?" said Zuzu.

SCRATCH, SCRATCH, SCRATCH!

Whatever it was, it wasn't giving up.

"We can't just sit here. Open the door, Frankie," whispered Zuzu.

"You open the door if you're so brave!" replied Frankie.

Zuzu quietly counted to three, then flung open the door.

"Oh!" she cried.

Chapter 2

Outside sat a small, scruffy dog with floppy ears. He wagged his tail, pleased to see them.

"Hello, doggy," said Zuzu. "Where did you come from?"

The dog barked.

The dog didn't seem scared of dragons at all. He let Zuzu tickle his tummy.

"What should we do with him?" asked Zuzu.

"I've no idea!" said Mrs Dragon.

"He needs a bath!" said Frankie, pinching his nose. "He must be hungry, too."

The Dragons did the only sensible thing. They gave the dog a bath and fed him. The dog's wet fur stood up like a hairbrush.

"We should call him Scruff," laughed Zuzu.

"He's not our dog," grumbled Grandpa.

"Perhaps he doesn't belong to anyone," said Frankie.

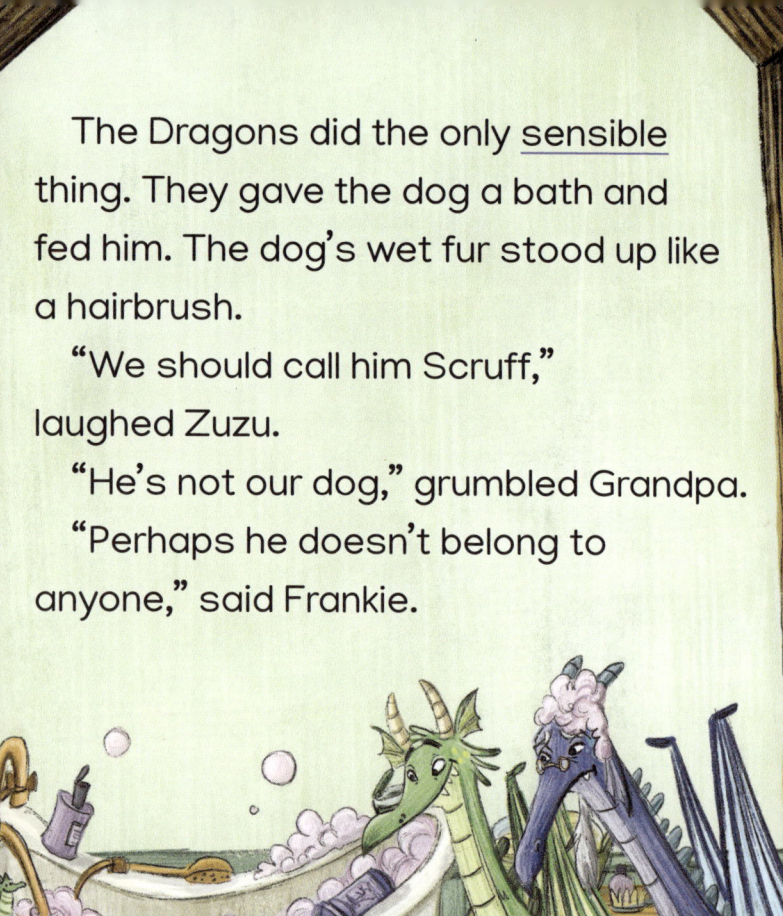

A sensible person or thing is wise or shows common sense.

Weeks went by ... no one came looking for the dog. Scruff made himself at home and developed his own new habits.

He slept in his warm bed.

He played chase in the garden with the twins.

He followed Mrs Dragon everywhere and chewed Grandpa's favourite slippers.

A habit is something that you do often.

Before long, Scruff was part of the family.

There was one problem, though. Scruff had a lot of energy. He needed to be walked.

"We can't take him out," worried Mrs Dragon. "People will see us!"

"Not if we go at night," suggested Zuzu.

Soon, midnight walks with Scruff became a new habit for the twins. It was an adventure to go out after dark. They kept away from the town and only met owls and rabbits. Scruff chased after the rabbits, but never caught a single one.

A habit is something that you do often.

 # Chapter 3

One morning, Zuzu woke up and looked for Scruff. He wasn't curled up at the foot of her bed as usual. Outside the wind moaned. Rain drummed on the roof.

Zuzu shook Frankie awake. "Where's Scruff?" she asked.

"Isn't he with you?" asked Frankie.

They searched the whole house. Zuzu even looked up the chimney. Scruff was nowhere to be found.

Then Zuzu noticed the front door. It was half open. Scruff must have escaped.

"Did you close the door after our walk?" asked Zuzu.

"Yes!" said Frankie. "Wait … oh, I don't remember."

They called Scruff's name into the wind.

"I'm sure he'll come back soon," said Mrs Dragon.

"Wait a while," suggested Grandpa.

"We can't leave him out in this rain!" Zuzu cried. "He might be lost."

"Maybe he ran off to the town," said Mrs Dragon.

"Then I'll just have to find him," said Zuzu.

"We'll find him," said Frankie. "I'm coming with you."

Mrs Dragon tried to convince them to wait, but the twins were determined to go.

In the end, she gave them an umbrella.

"Don't talk to people," Mrs Dragon warned. "Remember, they'll only scream and run away."

To convince someone is to persuade them about something.

Before they left, Zuzu had an idea. She made a poster with a picture of Scruff to show to anyone they met. She put it in her pocket.

 Chapter 4

The twins set off down the muddy track. Frankie linked arms with his sister.

"What if the people yell at us or chase us away?" Frankie asked.

"They might not," said Zuzu. "Anyway, we have to find Scruff."

To link things is to join them together.

The rain had reduced to a drizzle.

Before long, they came to a row of tall, white houses.

A woman rode up the street on her bike.

"Let's ask this woman if she's seen Scruff," said Zuzu.

If something reduces or is reduced, it gets smaller in size or amount.

"Excuse me," said Zuzu.

The woman took one look at them and gasped. She wobbled and fell off her bike.

Then she ran off, screaming. "Dragons! Help!" she shouted.

Zuzu and Frankie looked at each other. Their ma was right. Maybe it was better to stay at home.

At last, the rain stopped and the sun came out. The twins reached a park where children were playing.

Frankie and Zuzu approached them carefully, making the minimum amount of noise.

Unfortunately, a girl spotted them. "D-D-Dragons!" she screamed. "Run!"

A minimum of something is the least or smallest amount possible.

In seconds, everyone had run away. The park was empty – or so the twins thought.

One small boy had been left behind. He clung to the top of the climbing frame and started to wail.

"Waaah!" the boy cried.

"It's all right. Don't cry," said Zuzu. "Are you stuck?"

The boy nodded. His lip wobbled.

"Climb onto my back. I'll help you down," offered Zuzu.

Zuzu helped the boy safely to the ground.

"Zuzu, look!" whispered Frankie.

Some people were creeping back to the park. A girl ran over and took the boy's hand.

"This is my little brother, Kiran," she said. "Are you really dragons?"

Zuzu nodded. "I'm Zuzu and this is Frankie. We need your help," she said.

Zuzu showed them the poster.
"I've seen that dog in the square," said Kiran's sister.

The twins rushed to the square. They heard a bark they knew.

"Scruff!" cried Frankie.

Scruff was wet and muddy, but he was delighted to see them.

Zuzu and Frankie returned to the park with their new friends. They gave the children rides on their backs.

People came out of their houses to watch.

"Perhaps we were wrong about dragons," they said. "They're not scary at all."

Some time later, Zuzu and Frankie set off home with Scruff.

"That was fun!" beamed Frankie.

"Yes," said Zuzu. "Let's take Scruff for a walk in the park tomorrow."

They couldn't wait to tell Ma and Grandpa about their adventure. Maybe people and dragons did mix, after all!

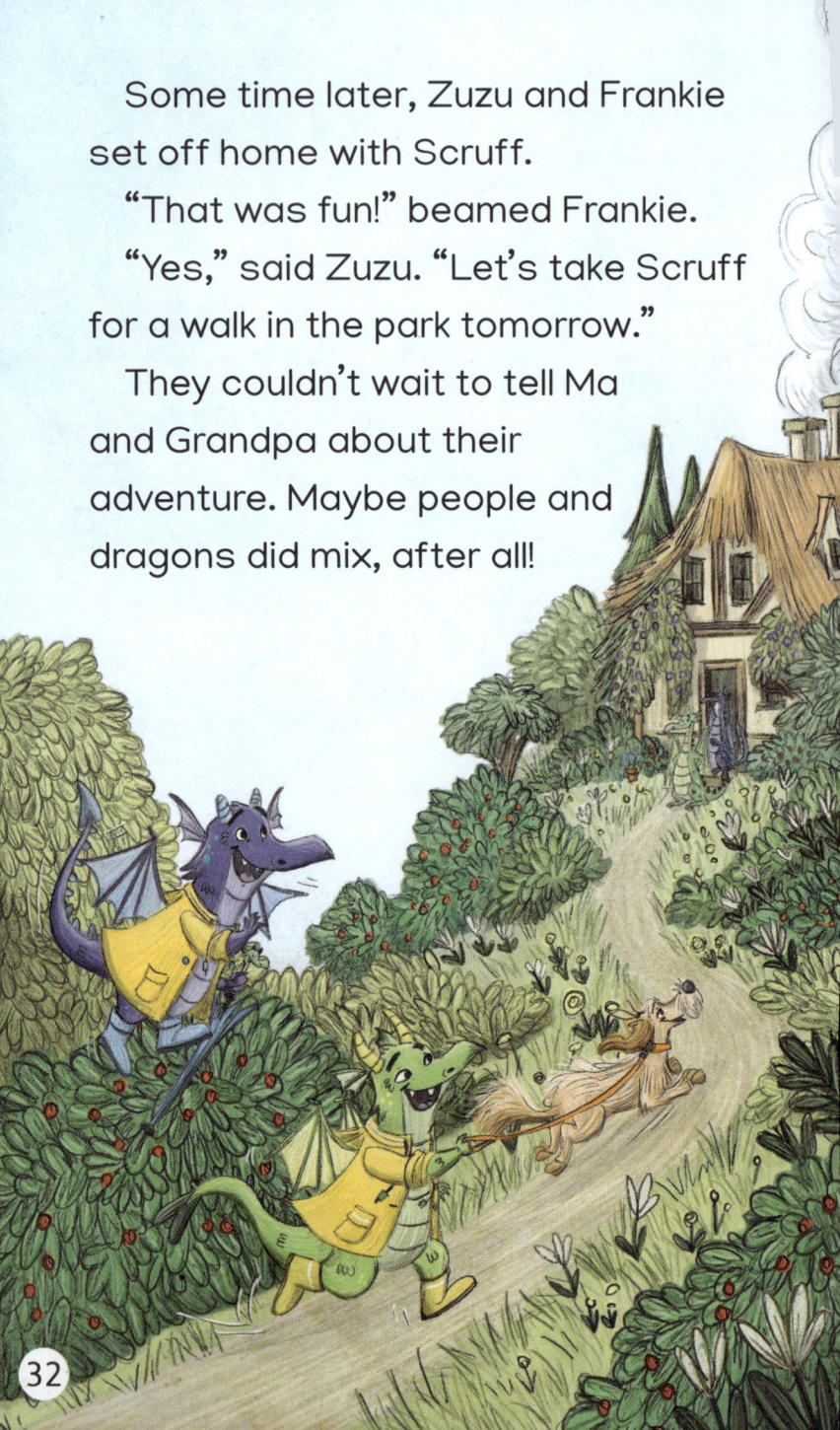